NAMES OF
Christ

WWW.THEREDHEADEDHOSTESS.COM

Table of Contents

see also atonement, mediator

DEFINITION OF THIS NAME: intercession

Someone who publicly supports or recommends
Someone who pleads a case on another's behalf.
Christ is the advocate with the Father on
behalf of the righteous

SCRIPTURES THIS NAME IS USED	WHAT THE SCRIPTURE SAYS
1 JOHN 2:1	Christ is the advocate with the Father
Moro 7:28	He has answered the ends of the law He advocateth the cause of the children of men
D&C 45:3-5	He pleads our cause with the Father because he suffered for us. Spare those who believe
110:4	1st & last, he lives, he was slain
Heb 7:25	He ever liveth to make intercession for them

WHY CHRIST HAS THIS NAME

Because Christ was perfect & able to atone
for our sins he is uniquely qualified
to plead to the Father in our behalf.
He takes and cleanses us from sin
and allows us to be worthy to be
back in Father's presence

Why does Christ needs to advocate before a perfect Elohim?

My salvation is dependent upon Christ's atonement. Without His payment for my sins I would never be worthy of eternal life. For some reason Christ needs to plead for me before the Father.

How can the advocacy of Christ inspire us to extend mercy and forgiveness to others?

D&C 62:1 He is advocate, knows our weakness & how to succor
D&C 29:5 Rejoice Be glad that he is advocate
Mos 15:8 Victory over death gives son power to make intercession

ALMIGHTY

DEFINITION OF THIS NAME:

Having complete power
A name or title for God
Omnipotent

SCRIPTURES THIS NAME IS USED	WHAT THE SCRIPTURE SAYS
REVELATION 1:8	alpha & Omega, names for Christ
Mosiah 3:5	Lord Omnipotent will live come down & on earth
Gen 17:1	Lord appeared to Abram calling himself Almighty God
Moses 1:3	Introduces himself to Moses
John 3:35	God has given all things into Christ's hand

WHY CHRIST HAS THIS NAME

Elohim has given Christ all power.
He has power to save the Israelites
from the Egyptians with miracles
He empowered Nephi to build a ship
He redeemed me from sin
He will resurrect me.
He can exalt me

See TG: Jesus Christ, Power of; God,
power of, Jesus Christ, authority of

I owe everything to Heavenly Father
and Christ.
There is no miracle too big for him
There is nothing He can't do.

I can depend on Him
He will always do what He says He
will do.

Alpha and Omega

Definition of This Name:

Scriptures this Name is Used	What the scripture says
Revelation 1:8	

Why Christ has this Name

INSIGHTS THIS NAME GIVES ME ABOUT CHRIST AND MY RELATIONSHIP
WITH HIM:

AMEN

Definition of This Name:

_____

_____

_____

Scriptures this Name is Used	What the scripture says
Revelation 3:14	

Why Christ has this Name

_____

_____

_____

_____

_____

_____

_____

_____

_____

INSIGHTS THIS NAME GIVES ME ABOUT CHRIST AND MY RELATIONSHIP WITH HIM:

APOSTLE

DEFINITION OF THIS NAME:

SCRIPTURES THIS NAME IS USED	WHAT THE SCRIPTURE SAYS
HEBREWS 3:1	

WHY CHRIST HAS THIS NAME

INSIGHTS THIS NAME GIVES ME ABOUT CHRIST AND MY RELATIONSHIP WITH HIM:

AUTHOR

Definition of This Name:

_____

_____

_____

Scriptures this Name is Used	What the scripture says
Hebrews 5:9	

Why Christ has this Name

_____

_____

_____

_____

_____

_____

_____

_____

INSIGHTS THIS NAME GIVES ME ABOUT CHRIST AND MY RELATIONSHIP WITH HIM:

BELOVED

DEFINITION OF THIS NAME:

SCRIPTURES THIS NAME IS USED	WHAT THE SCRIPTURE SAYS
LUKE 9:35	

WHY CHRIST HAS THIS NAME

INSIGHTS THIS NAME GIVES ME ABOUT CHRIST AND MY RELATIONSHIP
WITH HIM:

BRANCH

Definition of This Name:

Scriptures this Name is Used	What the scripture says
Jeremiah 23:5	

Why Christ has this Name

INSIGHTS THIS NAME GIVES ME ABOUT CHRIST AND MY RELATIONSHIP
WITH HIM:

BREAD OF LIFE

DEFINITION OF THIS NAME:

_____

_____

_____

SCRIPTURES THIS NAME IS USED	WHAT THE SCRIPTURE SAYS
JOHN 6:48	

WHY CHRIST HAS THIS NAME

_____

_____

_____

_____

_____

_____

_____

_____

_____

INSIGHTS THIS NAME GIVES ME ABOUT CHRIST AND MY RELATIONSHIP WITH HIM:

BRIDEGROOM

DEFINITION OF THIS NAME:

SCRIPTURES THIS NAME IS USED	WHAT THE SCRIPTURE SAYS
MATTHEW 25:1	

WHY CHRIST HAS THIS NAME

Insights this name gives me about Christ and my relationship
with him:

BRIGHT AND MORNING STAR

DEFINITION OF THIS NAME:

SCRIPTURES THIS NAME IS USED	WHAT THE SCRIPTURE SAYS
REVELATION 22:16	

WHY CHRIST HAS THIS NAME

INSIGHTS THIS NAME GIVES ME ABOUT CHRIST AND MY RELATIONSHIP
WITH HIM:

CAPTAIN OF SALVATION

DEFINITION OF THIS NAME:

SCRIPTURES THIS NAME IS USED	WHAT THE SCRIPTURE SAYS
HEBREWS 2:10	

WHY CHRIST HAS THIS NAME

INSIGHTS THIS NAME GIVES ME ABOUT CHRIST AND MY RELATIONSHIP WITH HIM:

CARPENTER

Definition of This Name:

Scriptures this Name is Used	What the scripture says
MARK 6:3	

Why Christ has this Name

INSIGHTS THIS NAME GIVES ME ABOUT CHRIST AND MY RELATIONSHIP
WITH HIM:

CHIEF CORNERSTONE

Definition of This Name:

_____
_____
_____

Scriptures this Name is Used	What the scripture says
Ephesians 2:20	

Why Christ has this Name

_____
_____
_____
_____
_____
_____
_____
_____
_____

INSIGHTS THIS NAME GIVES ME ABOUT CHRIST AND MY RELATIONSHIP
WITH HIM:

CHIEF SHEPHERD

DEFINITION OF THIS NAME:

SCRIPTURES THIS NAME IS USED	WHAT THE SCRIPTURE SAYS
1 PETER 5:4	

WHY CHRIST HAS THIS NAME

INSIGHTS THIS NAME GIVES ME ABOUT CHRIST AND MY RELATIONSHIP
WITH HIM:

CHRIST

Definition of This Name:

_____

_____

_____

Scriptures this Name is Used	What the scripture says
Matthew 16:16	

Why Christ has this Name

_____

_____

_____

_____

_____

_____

_____

_____

_____

INSIGHTS THIS NAME GIVES ME ABOUT CHRIST AND MY RELATIONSHIP
WITH HIM:

COMMANDER

DEFINITION OF THIS NAME:

_____

_____

_____

SCRIPTURES THIS NAME IS USED	WHAT THE SCRIPTURE SAYS
ISAIAH 55:4	

WHY CHRIST HAS THIS NAME

_____

_____

_____

_____

_____

_____

_____

_____

_____

INSIGHTS THIS NAME GIVES ME ABOUT CHRIST AND MY RELATIONSHIP
WITH HIM:

COUNSELOR

DEFINITION OF THIS NAME:

SCRIPTURES THIS NAME IS USED	WHAT THE SCRIPTURE SAYS
ISAIAH 9:6	

WHY CHRIST HAS THIS NAME

INSIGHTS THIS NAME GIVES ME ABOUT CHRIST AND MY RELATIONSHIP WITH HIM:

CREATOR

DEFINITION OF THIS NAME:

SCRIPTURES THIS NAME IS USED	WHAT THE SCRIPTURE SAYS
ISAIAH 40:28	

WHY CHRIST HAS THIS NAME

INSIGHTS THIS NAME GIVES ME ABOUT CHRIST AND MY RELATIONSHIP
WITH HIM:

Deliverer

DEFINITION OF THIS NAME:

SCRIPTURES THIS NAME IS USED	WHAT THE SCRIPTURE SAYS
PSALMS 18:2	

WHY CHRIST HAS THIS NAME

INSIGHTS THIS NAME GIVES ME ABOUT CHRIST AND MY RELATIONSHIP WITH HIM:

DOOR

DEFINITION OF THIS NAME:

SCRIPTURES THIS NAME IS USED	WHAT THE SCRIPTURE SAYS
JOHN 10:7	

WHY CHRIST HAS THIS NAME

INSIGHTS THIS NAME GIVES ME ABOUT CHRIST AND MY RELATIONSHIP
WITH HIM:

EVERLASTING FATHER

DEFINITION OF THIS NAME:

SCRIPTURES THIS NAME IS USED	WHAT THE SCRIPTURE SAYS
ISAIAH 9:6	

WHY CHRIST HAS THIS NAME

INSIGHTS THIS NAME GIVES ME ABOUT CHRIST AND MY RELATIONSHIP WITH HIM:

First and Last

Definition of This Name:

_____

_____

_____

Scriptures this Name is Used	What the scripture says
Revelation 22:13	

Why Christ has this Name

_____

_____

_____

_____

_____

_____

_____

_____

_____

INSIGHTS THIS NAME GIVES ME ABOUT CHRIST AND MY RELATIONSHIP WITH HIM:

Firstborn

Definition of This Name:

_____

_____

_____

Scriptures this Name is Used	What the scripture says
Hebrews 12:23	

Why Christ has this Name

_____

_____

_____

_____

_____

_____

_____

_____

_____

INSIGHTS THIS NAME GIVES ME ABOUT CHRIST AND MY RELATIONSHIP WITH HIM:

GOD

DEFINITION OF THIS NAME:

SCRIPTURES THIS NAME IS USED	WHAT THE SCRIPTURE SAYS
ISAIAH 51:15	

WHY CHRIST HAS THIS NAME

INSIGHTS THIS NAME GIVES ME ABOUT CHRIST AND MY RELATIONSHIP WITH HIM:

GOOD SHEPHERD

DEFINITION OF THIS NAME:

_____

_____

_____

SCRIPTURES THIS NAME IS USED	WHAT THE SCRIPTURE SAYS
JOHN 10:11	

WHY CHRIST HAS THIS NAME

_____

_____

_____

_____

_____

_____

_____

_____

INSIGHTS THIS NAME GIVES ME ABOUT CHRIST AND MY RELATIONSHIP
WITH HIM:

GOVERNOR

Definition of This Name:

_____

_____

_____

Scriptures this Name is Used	What the scripture says
Matthew 2:6	

Why Christ has this Name

_____

_____

_____

_____

_____

_____

_____

_____

_____

INSIGHTS THIS NAME GIVES ME ABOUT CHRIST AND MY RELATIONSHIP
WITH HIM:

Great High Priest

DEFINITION OF THIS NAME:

SCRIPTURES this Name is Used	What the scripture says
Hebrews 4:14	

WHY CHRIST HAS THIS NAME

INSIGHTS THIS NAME GIVES ME ABOUT CHRIST AND MY RELATIONSHIP
WITH HIM:

HOLY CHILD

Definition of This Name:

_____

_____

_____

Scriptures this Name is Used	What the scripture says
ACTS 4:30	

Why Christ has this Name

_____

_____

_____

_____

_____

_____

_____

_____

INSIGHTS THIS NAME GIVES ME ABOUT CHRIST AND MY RELATIONSHIP WITH HIM:

I Am

DEFINITION OF THIS NAME:

SCRIPTURES THIS NAME IS USED	WHAT THE SCRIPTURE SAYS
EXODUS 3:14	

WHY CHRIST HAS THIS NAME

INSIGHTS THIS NAME GIVES ME ABOUT CHRIST AND MY RELATIONSHIP
WITH HIM:

IMMANUEL

DEFINITION OF THIS NAME:

SCRIPTURES this Name is Used	WHAT THE SCRIPTURE SAYS
ISAIAH 7:14	

WHY CHRIST HAS THIS NAME

INSIGHTS THIS NAME GIVES ME ABOUT CHRIST AND MY RELATIONSHIP WITH HIM:

JESUS

DEFINITION OF THIS NAME:

SCRIPTURES THIS NAME IS USED	WHAT THE SCRIPTURE SAYS
MATTHEW 1:21	

WHY CHRIST HAS THIS NAME

INSIGHTS THIS NAME GIVES ME ABOUT CHRIST AND MY RELATIONSHIP
WITH HIM:

JESUS THE CHRIST

DEFINITION OF THIS NAME:

SCRIPTURES THIS NAME IS USED	WHAT THE SCRIPTURE SAYS
MATTHEW 16:20	

WHY CHRIST HAS THIS NAME

INSIGHTS THIS NAME GIVES ME ABOUT CHRIST AND MY RELATIONSHIP
WITH HIM:

JESUS OF NAZARETH

DEFINITION OF THIS NAME:

SCRIPTURES THIS NAME IS USED	WHAT THE SCRIPTURE SAYS
JOHN 18:7	

WHY CHRIST HAS THIS NAME

INSIGHTS THIS NAME GIVES ME ABOUT CHRIST AND MY RELATIONSHIP
WITH HIM:

JUDGE

DEFINITION OF THIS NAME:

SCRIPTURES this NAME is USED	WHAT THE SCRIPTURE SAYS
PSALMS 96:13	

WHY CHRIST HAS THIS NAME

INSIGHTS THIS NAME GIVES ME ABOUT CHRIST AND MY RELATIONSHIP
WITH HIM:

JUST ONE

DEFINITION OF THIS NAME:

SCRIPTURES THIS NAME IS USED	WHAT THE SCRIPTURE SAYS
ACTS 7:52	

WHY CHRIST HAS THIS NAME

INSIGHTS THIS NAME GIVES ME ABOUT CHRIST AND MY RELATIONSHIP WITH HIM:

KING

Definition of This Name:

_____

_____

_____

Scriptures this Name is Used	What the scripture says
John 19:21	

Why Christ has this Name

_____

_____

_____

_____

_____

_____

_____

_____

_____

INSIGHTS THIS NAME GIVES ME ABOUT CHRIST AND MY RELATIONSHIP WITH HIM:

KING OF KINGS

DEFINITION OF THIS NAME:

SCRIPTURES THIS NAME IS USED	WHAT THE SCRIPTURE SAYS
REVELATION 17:14	

WHY CHRIST HAS THIS NAME

INSIGHTS THIS NAME GIVES ME ABOUT CHRIST AND MY RELATIONSHIP WITH HIM:

LAMB OF GOD

DEFINITION OF THIS NAME:

SCRIPTURES THIS NAME IS USED	WHAT THE SCRIPTURE SAYS
JOHN 1:36	

WHY CHRIST HAS THIS NAME

INSIGHTS THIS NAME GIVES ME ABOUT CHRIST AND MY RELATIONSHIP
WITH HIM:

LAWGIVER

Definition of This Name:

Scriptures this Name is Used	What the scripture says
Isaiah 33:22	

Why Christ has this Name

INSIGHTS THIS NAME GIVES ME ABOUT CHRIST AND MY RELATIONSHIP
WITH HIM:

DEFINITION OF THIS NAME:

Scriptures / What the scripture says

SCRIPTURES THIS NAME IS USED	WHAT THE SCRIPTURE SAYS
ISAIAH 55:4	

WHY CHRIST HAS THIS NAME

INSIGHTS THIS NAME GIVES ME ABOUT CHRIST AND MY RELATIONSHIP
WITH HIM:

LIFE

DEFINITION OF THIS NAME:

SCRIPTURES THIS NAME IS USED	WHAT THE SCRIPTURE SAYS
JOHN 14:6	

WHY CHRIST HAS THIS NAME

INSIGHTS THIS NAME GIVES ME ABOUT CHRIST AND MY RELATIONSHIP
WITH HIM:

LIGHT OF THE WORLD

DEFINITION OF THIS NAME:

_____

_____

_____

SCRIPTURES THIS NAME IS USED	WHAT THE SCRIPTURE SAYS
JOHN 8:12	

WHY CHRIST HAS THIS NAME

_____

_____

_____

_____

_____

_____

_____

_____

_____

INSIGHTS THIS NAME GIVES ME ABOUT CHRIST AND MY RELATIONSHIP
WITH HIM:

LION OF THE TRIBE OF JUDAH

DEFINITION OF THIS NAME:

SCRIPTURES THIS NAME IS USED	WHAT THE SCRIPTURE SAYS
REVELATION 5:5	

WHY CHRIST HAS THIS NAME

INSIGHTS THIS NAME GIVES ME ABOUT CHRIST AND MY RELATIONSHIP
WITH HIM:

LIVING BREAD

DEFINITION OF THIS NAME:

SCRIPTURES THIS NAME IS USED	WHAT THE SCRIPTURE SAYS
JOHN 6:51	

WHY CHRIST HAS THIS NAME

INSIGHTS THIS NAME GIVES ME ABOUT CHRIST AND MY RELATIONSHIP
WITH HIM:

LIVING STONE

DEFINITION OF THIS NAME:

SCRIPTURES THIS NAME IS USED	WHAT THE SCRIPTURE SAYS
1 PETER 2:4	

WHY CHRIST HAS THIS NAME

INSIGHTS THIS NAME GIVES ME ABOUT CHRIST AND MY RELATIONSHIP WITH HIM:

LORD

DEFINITION OF THIS NAME:

SCRIPTURES THIS NAME IS USED	WHAT THE SCRIPTURE SAYS
JOHN 6:68	

WHY CHRIST HAS THIS NAME

INSIGHTS THIS NAME GIVES ME ABOUT CHRIST AND MY RELATIONSHIP
WITH HIM:

LORD OF HOSTS

DEFINITION OF THIS NAME:

SCRIPTURES THIS NAME IS USED	WHAT THE SCRIPTURE SAYS
ISAIAH 44:6	

WHY CHRIST HAS THIS NAME

INSIGHTS THIS NAME GIVES ME ABOUT CHRIST AND MY RELATIONSHIP WITH HIM:

LORD OF LORDS

DEFINITION OF THIS NAME:

SCRIPTURES THIS NAME IS USED	WHAT THE SCRIPTURE SAYS
REVELATION 17:14	

WHY CHRIST HAS THIS NAME

INSIGHTS THIS NAME GIVES ME ABOUT CHRIST AND MY RELATIONSHIP
WITH HIM:

MAN OF SORROWS

DEFINITION OF THIS NAME:

SCRIPTURES THIS NAME IS USED	WHAT THE SCRIPTURE SAYS
ISAIAH 53:3	

WHY CHRIST HAS THIS NAME

INSIGHTS THIS NAME GIVES ME ABOUT CHRIST AND MY RELATIONSHIP
WITH HIM:

MEDIATOR

DEFINITION OF THIS NAME:

SCRIPTURES THIS NAME IS USED	WHAT THE SCRIPTURE SAYS
1 TIMOTHY 2:5	

WHY CHRIST HAS THIS NAME

INSIGHTS THIS NAME GIVES ME ABOUT CHRIST AND MY RELATIONSHIP WITH HIM:

Messiah

Definition of This Name:

Scriptures this Name is Used	What the scripture says
John 1:41	

Why Christ has this Name

INSIGHTS THIS NAME GIVES ME ABOUT CHRIST AND MY RELATIONSHIP
WITH HIM:

ONLY BEGOTTEN

DEFINITION OF THIS NAME:

SCRIPTURES THIS NAME IS USED	WHAT THE SCRIPTURE SAYS
JOHN 1:18	

WHY CHRIST HAS THIS NAME

INSIGHTS THIS NAME GIVES ME ABOUT CHRIST AND MY RELATIONSHIP WITH HIM:

OUR PASSOVER

DEFINITION OF THIS NAME:

SCRIPTURES THIS NAME IS USED	WHAT THE SCRIPTURE SAYS
1 CORINTHIANS 5:7	

WHY CHRIST HAS THIS NAME

INSIGHTS THIS NAME GIVES ME ABOUT CHRIST AND MY RELATIONSHIP
WITH HIM:

PRINCE OF PEACE

DEFINITION OF THIS NAME:

SCRIPTURES THIS NAME IS USED	WHAT THE SCRIPTURE SAYS
ISAIAH 9:6	

WHY CHRIST HAS THIS NAME

INSIGHTS THIS NAME GIVES ME ABOUT CHRIST AND MY RELATIONSHIP WITH HIM:

PROPHET

DEFINITION OF THIS NAME:

SCRIPTURES THIS NAME IS USED	WHAT THE SCRIPTURE SAYS
JOHN 7:40	

WHY CHRIST HAS THIS NAME

INSIGHTS THIS NAME GIVES ME ABOUT CHRIST AND MY RELATIONSHIP WITH HIM:

RABBI

DEFINITION OF THIS NAME:

SCRIPTURES THIS NAME IS USED	WHAT THE SCRIPTURE SAYS
JOHN 1:49	

WHY CHRIST HAS THIS NAME

INSIGHTS THIS NAME GIVES ME ABOUT CHRIST AND MY RELATIONSHIP
WITH HIM:

REDEEMER

DEFINITION OF THIS NAME:

SCRIPTURES THIS NAME IS USED	WHAT THE SCRIPTURE SAYS
JOB 19:25	

WHY CHRIST HAS THIS NAME

INSIGHTS THIS NAME GIVES ME ABOUT CHRIST AND MY RELATIONSHIP
WITH HIM:

RESURRECTION AND LIFE

DEFINITION OF THIS NAME:

SCRIPTURES THIS NAME IS USED	WHAT THE SCRIPTURE SAYS
JOHN 11:25	

WHY CHRIST HAS THIS NAME

INSIGHTS THIS NAME GIVES ME ABOUT CHRIST AND MY RELATIONSHIP WITH HIM:

ROCK

DEFINITION OF THIS NAME:

SCRIPTURES THIS NAME IS USED	WHAT THE SCRIPTURE SAYS
1 CORINTHIANS 10:4	

WHY CHRIST HAS THIS NAME

INSIGHTS THIS NAME GIVES ME ABOUT CHRIST AND MY RELATIONSHIP WITH HIM:

ROOT OF DAVID

DEFINITION OF THIS NAME:

SCRIPTURES THIS NAME IS USED	WHAT THE SCRIPTURE SAYS
REVELATION 5:5	

WHY CHRIST HAS THIS NAME

INSIGHTS THIS NAME GIVES ME ABOUT CHRIST AND MY RELATIONSHIP
WITH HIM:

SAVIOR

DEFINITION OF THIS NAME:

SCRIPTURES THIS NAME IS USED	WHAT THE SCRIPTURE SAYS
LUKE 1:47	

WHY CHRIST HAS THIS NAME

INSIGHTS THIS NAME GIVES ME ABOUT CHRIST AND MY RELATIONSHIP WITH HIM:

SHEPHERD

DEFINITION OF THIS NAME:

SCRIPTURES THIS NAME IS USED	WHAT THE SCRIPTURE SAYS
PSALMS 23:1	

WHY CHRIST HAS THIS NAME

INSIGHTS THIS NAME GIVES ME ABOUT CHRIST AND MY RELATIONSHIP WITH HIM:

SON OF GOD

DEFINITION OF THIS NAME:

_____

_____

_____

SCRIPTURES THIS NAME IS USED	WHAT THE SCRIPTURE SAYS
1 JOHN 4:15	

WHY CHRIST HAS THIS NAME

_____

_____

_____

_____

_____

_____

_____

_____

_____

INSIGHTS THIS NAME GIVES ME ABOUT CHRIST AND MY RELATIONSHIP WITH HIM:

SURE FOUNDATION

DEFINITION OF THIS NAME:

SCRIPTURES THIS NAME IS USED	WHAT THE SCRIPTURE SAYS
ISAIAH 28:16	

WHY CHRIST HAS THIS NAME

INSIGHTS THIS NAME GIVES ME ABOUT CHRIST AND MY RELATIONSHIP WITH HIM:

TEACHER

DEFINITION OF THIS NAME:

SCRIPTURES THIS NAME IS USED	WHAT THE SCRIPTURE SAYS
JOHN 3:2	

WHY CHRIST HAS THIS NAME

INSIGHTS THIS NAME GIVES ME ABOUT CHRIST AND MY RELATIONSHIP
WITH HIM:

TRUE LIGHT

DEFINITION OF THIS NAME:

SCRIPTURES THIS NAME IS USED	WHAT THE SCRIPTURE SAYS
JOHN 1:9	

WHY CHRIST HAS THIS NAME

INSIGHTS THIS NAME GIVES ME ABOUT CHRIST AND MY RELATIONSHIP WITH HIM:

True Vine

Definition of This Name:

Scriptures this Name is Used	What the scripture says
John 15:1	

Why Christ has this Name

INSIGHTS THIS NAME GIVES ME ABOUT CHRIST AND MY RELATIONSHIP WITH HIM:

WAY

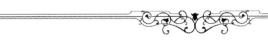

DEFINITION OF THIS NAME:

_____

_____

_____

SCRIPTURES THIS NAME IS USED	WHAT THE SCRIPTURE SAYS
JOHN 14:6	

WHY CHRIST HAS THIS NAME

_____

_____

_____

_____

_____

_____

_____

_____

INSIGHTS THIS NAME GIVES ME ABOUT CHRIST AND MY RELATIONSHIP WITH HIM:

WITNESS

Definition of This Name:

Scriptures this Name is Used	What the scripture says
Isaiah 55:4	

Why Christ has this Name

INSIGHTS THIS NAME GIVES ME ABOUT CHRIST AND MY RELATIONSHIP WITH HIM:

WONDERFUL

DEFINITION OF THIS NAME:

SCRIPTURES THIS NAME IS USED	**WHAT THE SCRIPTURE SAYS**
ISAIAH 9:6

WHY CHRIST HAS THIS NAME

INSIGHTS THIS NAME GIVES ME ABOUT CHRIST AND MY RELATIONSHIP
WITH HIM:

WORD

DEFINITION OF THIS NAME:

SCRIPTURES THIS NAME IS USED	WHAT THE SCRIPTURE SAYS
JOHN 1:1	

WHY CHRIST HAS THIS NAME

INSIGHTS THIS NAME GIVES ME ABOUT CHRIST AND MY RELATIONSHIP WITH HIM:

DEFINITION OF THIS NAME:

SCRIPTURES THIS NAME IS USED	WHAT THE SCRIPTURE SAYS

WHY CHRIST HAS THIS NAME

INSIGHTS THIS NAME GIVES ME ABOUT CHRIST AND MY RELATIONSHIP WITH HIM:

DEFINITION OF THIS NAME:

SCRIPTURES THIS NAME IS USED	WHAT THE SCRIPTURE SAYS

WHY CHRIST HAS THIS NAME

INSIGHTS THIS NAME GIVES ME ABOUT CHRIST AND MY RELATIONSHIP WITH HIM:

Definition of This Name:

_____

_____

_____

Scriptures this Name is Used	What the scripture says

Why Christ has this Name

_____

_____

_____

_____

_____

_____

_____

_____

_____

INSIGHTS THIS NAME GIVES ME ABOUT CHRIST AND MY RELATIONSHIP WITH HIM:

DEFINITION OF THIS NAME:

SCRIPTURES THIS NAME IS USED	WHAT THE SCRIPTURE SAYS

WHY CHRIST HAS THIS NAME

INSIGHTS THIS NAME GIVES ME ABOUT CHRIST AND MY RELATIONSHIP WITH HIM:

DEFINITION OF THIS NAME:

SCRIPTURES THIS NAME IS USED	WHAT THE SCRIPTURE SAYS

WHY CHRIST HAS THIS NAME

INSIGHTS THIS NAME GIVES ME ABOUT CHRIST AND MY RELATIONSHIP
WITH HIM:

DEFINITION OF THIS NAME:

SCRIPTURES THIS NAME IS USED	WHAT THE SCRIPTURE SAYS

WHY CHRIST HAS THIS NAME

INSIGHTS THIS NAME GIVES ME ABOUT CHRIST AND MY RELATIONSHIP
WITH HIM:

DEFINITION OF THIS NAME:

SCRIPTURES THIS NAME IS USED	WHAT THE SCRIPTURE SAYS

WHY CHRIST HAS THIS NAME

INSIGHTS THIS NAME GIVES ME ABOUT CHRIST AND MY RELATIONSHIP WITH HIM:

DEFINITION OF THIS NAME:

_____

_____

_____

SCRIPTURES THIS NAME IS USED	WHAT THE SCRIPTURE SAYS

WHY CHRIST HAS THIS NAME

_____

_____

_____

_____

_____

_____

_____

_____

_____

INSIGHTS THIS NAME GIVES ME ABOUT CHRIST AND MY RELATIONSHIP WITH HIM:

DEFINITION OF THIS NAME:

SCRIPTURES THIS NAME IS USED	WHAT THE SCRIPTURE SAYS

WHY CHRIST HAS THIS NAME

INSIGHTS THIS NAME GIVES ME ABOUT CHRIST AND MY RELATIONSHIP WITH HIM:

DEFINITION OF THIS NAME:

SCRIPTURES THIS NAME IS USED	WHAT THE SCRIPTURE SAYS

WHY CHRIST HAS THIS NAME

INSIGHTS THIS NAME GIVES ME ABOUT CHRIST AND MY RELATIONSHIP WITH HIM:

DEFINITION OF THIS NAME:

SCRIPTURES THIS NAME IS USED	WHAT THE SCRIPTURE SAYS

WHY CHRIST HAS THIS NAME

INSIGHTS THIS NAME GIVES ME ABOUT CHRIST AND MY RELATIONSHIP WITH HIM:

DEFINITION OF THIS NAME:

SCRIPTURES THIS NAME IS USED	WHAT THE SCRIPTURE SAYS

WHY CHRIST HAS THIS NAME

INSIGHTS THIS NAME GIVES ME ABOUT CHRIST AND MY RELATIONSHIP WITH HIM:

Made in the USA
Charleston, SC
04 December 2015